CROWDBREAKERS II

CROWDBREAKERS II

A powerpack of games for youth groups

BOB AND JILLY MOFFETT

Illustrated by Simon Jenkins

MarshallPickering
An Imprint of HarperCollins*Publishers*

Marshall Pickering is an Imprint of
HarperCollins*Religious*
Part of HarperCollins*Publishers*
77–85 Fulham Palace Road, London W6 8JB

First published in Great Britain
in 1993 by Marshall Pickering

1 3 5 7 9 10 8 6 4 2

A catalogue record for this book is
available from the British Library

ISBN 0 551 02573 5

Printed and bound in Great Britain by
HarperCollinsManufacturing Glasgow

Contents

Preface

Why have we waited so long to publish *Crowdbreakers II*? This book has been sitting around in the filing cabinet almost as long as *Crowdbreakers* has been in print!

To be honest, we had no incentive to pick the file out of the cabinet until we came off the circuit of telling other people how to do youth ministry, and got back into it ourselves.

For a few years we became experts without a constituency and dryness crept in. We were losing touch with young people, but we were still considered respectable enough people to say something from a platform! Then God intervened. He cleared us off to the Middle East and told us very clearly to get on with it and start our own group attached to a church in Cyprus. And this has enabled us to discover again the richness and hurt of getting alongside young people in their needs.

Back into the grind of creative weekly programming and the incessant daily telephone calls from the youth. And back to the incredible fulfilment of seeing young people come to faith and grow in ways that you couldn't believe possible.

So the manuscript came to light as a means of survival. We have made many changes, but our commitment to crowdbreakers as a way of introducing young people from all walks of life into an atmosphere of learning still stands. Crowdbreakers are a great leveller. Whoever you are, it's the same custard pie!

Our thanks go to Olga Tsinoglou, our colleague who has assisted us in the typing of the manuscript, and to the

1

many young people to whom this book is dedicated for surviving Friday nights and countless weekends.

Our thanks to Youth For Christ International and Youth For Christ USA who gave us the original inspiration to consider crowdbreakers as a means of communication with young people. Thanks goes to them also for some of the original material over the years, which like all good crowdbreakers get adapted by each practitioner.

Also our thanks go to those who have unknowingly given us the ideas just by a word or action they made, which set up a train of thought culminating in another messy, gruesome crowdbreaker. Thanks also to those who have passed us crowdbreakers on paper; we hope you haven't infringed copyright!

As we all know, FOOD attracts youth like bees to jam. Jilly has used this ploy successfully for years. When the programme is over and the real relational session begins it's the simple food that encourages them to hang round and chat. So we've included a few easy recipes.

Included also are two sketches written by Michael and Richard Ramsden (Ramsden and Ramsden). Nursery stories are great for bringing out the profound and the child in people, and Michael and Richard have a slightly different approach to *The Three Bears* and *The Three Little Pigs*. Although it may be X-certificate stuff, with a little practice it goes down well.

So the book has been produced on the whole by big kids called youth leaders doing what is termed 'youth ministry'. The material has been picked up along the way. And sometimes you will even find an original idea!

Bob and Jilly Moffett
Spring 1992

Crowdbreakers Explained

'We begin our study this evening in the third book of the second prophet of the first king of the sixteenth era of Palestine.'

Meanwhile half of the youth members have already gone out to the chippy, while the other half have pressed their instant mobile emergency button to tune their ears to their walkmans and are listening to the latest hits.

Jesus seemed to take people from the *potential* to the *possibility* and he did this by leading them from the little they knew and could see to earth-shattering conclusions. The Sermon on the Mount is full of such beautiful stories, taking people from where they are to where Jesus wanted them to be.

And now, reading from the first Book of Eliphazzzzzzz

When they arrive at your youth meeting after a day at school, an argument with their parents or almost getting knocked over by a car outside your home, the young people may not be in an ideal mood to study the Scriptures or to take part in a serious discussion of eternal commitment. So let me give you a few good reasons why crowdbreakers should be part of your programme.

Crowdbreakers create the right atmosphere

- Crowdbreakers relax both the young people and the leader, creating a congenial atmosphere in which communication can take place.

- Crowdbreakers get young people rubbing shoulders with each other—with people they naturally enjoy and know, and also with those they may dislike.

- Crowdbreakers give young people good, healthy, creative fun.

- Crowdbreakers create opportunities to meet members of the opposite sex within a sociable framework that is not pressurised, and to practise and develop social skills.

- Crowdbreakers break down the normal cliques that are formed in any group and pave the way for discussions which can lead to discovery of new concepts and truth.

- Crowdbreakers prepare a young person to experience a theme subject before considering it within a teaching format.

- Crowdbreakers allow for positive group control, and can assist in more effective discipline.

- Crowdbreakers build rapport between the leader and the group. The leader is seen as a wholesome, all-round type of person who enjoys having fun, as well as someone who can be serious and talk with care and understanding about God.

- Crowdbreakers reveal how each young person reacts in different game situations. When their guard is down, the leader can glimpse the other side of their character.

- Crowdbreakers give opportunities to create a positive image amongst un-churched young people, in place of negative images of Christianity as dull, boring and outmoded.

Crowdbreakers need planning

- Crowdbreakers should be read through very carefully so that you not only understand them, but also know exactly what could go wrong. Murphy's law states that 'if anything can go wrong, it will go wrong' at the worst moment for all concerned leaving you in the most embarrassing position.

- Crowdbreakers need to appear spontaneous. I firmly believe in spontaneity as long as it is planned!

- Crowdbreakers on paper are usually very different at the moment you use them. Your plans and expectations can be scuttled by the failure of your young people to participate and react in the way you expect. Be prepared.

- Crowdbreakers require preparation and practice with equipment prior to the meeting. Make all of your assistants aware of the crowdbreakers as well.

- Crowdbreakers have a habit of destroying such things as Ming vases – usually in the home of your worst enemy – so be careful where you have your meeting and remove all breakables. Remember Murphy!

Programming with crowdbreakers

- Crowdbreakers should be used thematically. Choose your subject, then prepare two or three crowdbreakers to prepare your group for the topic.

- Crowdbreakers should involve as many of the young people as possible. Not all the crowdbreakers require every participant to play an active role, but those sitting on the sidelines must feel totally involved.

Crowdbreakers and you!

- Crowdbreakers are great but we need to be 'as wise as snakes and as harmless as doves'. Enthusiasm can lead us beyond what is understood as good taste, and our standards of good, clean, healthy fun may not always agree with those of all the parents or young people.

- Crowdbreakers do not work unless you are enthusiastic. Act as if you need to play the next crowdbreaker like you need the next breath. They need to see you as excited as they want to feel.

- Crowdbreakers are not just a means to an end; they should be enjoyed for their own sake. But they are a means to an end as well, for we want them to introduce a topic of importance. Be prepared to work at that connection. Like parables they should at times stand on their own.

- Crowdbreakers demand our commitment to *pray* that the interaction will enable our young people to participate freely in seeking out biblical truth in a congenial atmosphere. Our aim is God-given creativity for his glory.

- Crowdbreakers require your sensitivity. Don't place youngsters in a position they can't handle unless you know exactly what you are doing with their emotions. Never manipulate or use a crowdbreaker to be vindictive.

- Crowdbreakers sometimes require peer pressure to get your volunteer to participate. Encourage the group to applaud the reluctant volunteer. But never mock, or you will give the message that mocking is acceptable.

- Crowdbreakers must not drag. Your timing should leave the young people wishing that it had gone on just a little longer. Stopping when you are winning allows you to repeat a crowdbreaker another time.

- Crowdbreakers will go wrong for you sometimes, so always be ready to jump in with another quick 'unplanned' activity to dig yourself out of the hole!

- Crowdbreakers sometimes require you to prepare a couple of young people in advance so that they know how to react. This is a legitimate way to involve a young person, particularly if the crowdbreaker is messy.

- Crowdbreakers are only as new as you make them. Don't be afraid of adapting old ones and making up new ones. Most crowdbreakers in this book are ones

I have seen in action or old ones I have adapted to give them that little bit of extra spice.

Crowdbreakers in use

Crowdbreakers need your sensitive touch. No group is the same and your understanding of what does or does not work is a skill to be learnt. Jot down notes to remind you what date you used it and what adaptations you recommend for next time.

Crowdbreakers is not a book to be passed round the other leaders. It can become a personal record of your ideas and adaptations.

CROWDBREAKERS

1 Up the Garden Path

Lay out an obstacle course in a hall, garden or field. You could include tyres to climb through, rugs or tarpaulins to crawl under, etc. As the young people will be blindfolded, avoid any obviously hazardous obstacles. Tie some string between the objects to act as a guide.

Arrange your group into teams of four or five and walk them blindfold round the course. They should appoint their own leader who is simply the one in front with a blindfold as well!

Although everyone is blindfolded they should keep together finding their way past, through and round all the objects. You could tie the teams together with string attached to ankles, waist or wrists.

Time each team to determine the winner. The losers have to do the whole obstacle course backwards, with all the other teams watching and wailing with delight.

Played outside or inside

Guidance   Blindness   Dependence

EQUIPMENT: BLINDFOLDS, STRING, OBSTACLES

② Familiarity

Very simple. If you are using the same venue for all or most of your activities simply remove or change around a number of pictures, chairs and articles. The object of this game is simply observation. Each person or team must spot the changes and write them down.

The penalty for having the fewest changes listed is the job of putting everything back in its original place.

'Spinning Tray' is a similar game.

Played inside

Familiarity   Observation   Change   Church

EQUIPMENT: PAPER, PENS

(3) Spinning Tray

This is a well-worn but fun activity which is easy to set up.

Place 25 to 30 objects on a tray. They should be everyday articles which are familiar to your young people: a paper clip, toothbrush, comb, toilet roll, book, etc.

Give them just 30 seconds to view these objects while you spin the tray or carefully turn it round. Don't give comments during this time, particularly to explain any peculiar article which you have included for extra interest!

After 30 seconds they are given two minutes for each person to write a list of the objects which by now have been removed or covered.

The moment of truth. You now reveal the articles and shout them out to the pleasure of some and frustration of others.

This is a very quick but effective crowdbreaker.

Played inside

Observation   Church   Familiarity

EQUIPMENT: PAPER, PENS, A TRAY FULL OF OBJECTS

4 Drain-pipe Dream

The length of plastic guttering and the amount of ice cream you need for this depends entirely on the number of people in your group!

Join the lengths of pipe with guttering clips, and place some plastic sheeting underneath. Now deposit into it: ice cream, sliced bananas, chopped nuts, chocolate sauces, etc. All the group are then invited at the end of the 10 – 9 – 8 . . . 1 countdown to eat as much as they can. Using spoons normally helps in this game.

You may wish to place the guttering on tables to make it easier, or you may prefer to place it on the floor so they eat like animals!

We've just been playing Drain-pipe Dream...

14

Warning: This is messy but great!

Suggestion: Why not join with other groups and go for the longest banana split in the world? Our record is 10 metres of pipe stuck together – it was yuk!

Played inside
or outside

Gluttony Sharing
Fellowship

EQUIPMENT: A LENGTH OF PLASTIC GUTTERING, PLASTIC SHEETING, ICE CREAM, BANANAS, ICE CREAM TOPPINGS, SPOONS

5 Frogs' Legs

Increasingly our shops are stocking a wider variety of food. This old favourite is not so much a game as a social function.

Like all crowdbreakers it is important to pay attention to the environment in which the activity is to be played. Decorate the room with balloons to give a festive feel and, if you can get them from travel agents, display posters and flags from different countries . . . including a couple of foreign flags set up outside the door as people come in.

Set out delicacies of an international variety – not large quantities but small 'tasters'. This does not have to be very expensive. Label all the foods with a letter. Each person has to taste all the foods and put the name of a country against the letter. The winner is the person who guesses the most countries' foods, and his prize is to choose which dish he wishes to finish. A vote is taken on the worst tasting dish, which the loser has to eat.

If you are tackling the theme of 'race' you could use this poem.

> When I was born I was black.
> When I was grown up I was black.
> When I was ill I was black.
> When I was in the sun I was black.
> When I was dead I was black.
>
> but you
>
> When you were born you were pink.
> When you were grown up you were white.

When you were ill you were green.
When you were in the sun you were red.
When you were dead you were purple.

. . . and you have the nerve to call me coloured!

(Anon)

Played inside or outside

Race   Church Worldwide   Differences   Culture

⑥ A Game Not to Do

On a camp with Christians and non-Christians lead a Bible study on the Second Coming of Christ. In the middle of the night all the Christians disappear – leaders' meals left half eaten, washing-up left, toothbrush on the floor, etc.

Seriously, if you did this, you would have to come clean within minutes if not seconds!

Played outside

Terror   Second Coming of Christ

EQUIPMENT: NONE

7 Nowhere

Arrange for your group to be blindfolded or taken in a closed van to a destination unknown to any of them. From the drop-off point they are to make their way back to base, with only a compass and a whistle. If you are concerned about the capabilities of your group, follow on foot at a safe distance or stay with them but only as an observer.

Caution: Obviously this game has many potential dangers including weather conditions; food supplies, terrain, group abilities, etc.

This is a great team game, particularly if you drop teams off at equal distances from a central base.

Played outside

Endurance Adventure Initiative Challenge Fellowship

EQUIPMENT: NONE

8 Baked Bean Binge

Everybody sits in a circle. The first person challenges the person on the left to do something which the challenger *has* to be able to do, but doesn't think anybody else can do. If unable to do it, that person has to eat a spoonful of *cold* beans. If he or she can do it, the challenger has to eat the beans.

The person on the left now has the opportunity to place a challenge to the next person on the left with the same consequences.

It's a brilliant way of getting to know obscure things about your young people and giving them the opportunity to interact.

Played inside or outside

Peculiarities   Gifts   Abilities

EQUIPMENT: BAKED BEANS

9 Angels and Mortals

This brilliant crowdbreaker is probably the best in the book. Those of you who have played it will know what we mean.

Write the names of your young people on pieces of paper and put the names in a hat. Each person takes out a name and, assuming that it is not his or her own, keeps it and does not in any circumstances including torture reveal this name to anyone else! If you or they wish, they can simply memorize the name and then pass it to you for destruction . . . you must not look at it either.

For the next four weeks each person attempts to be an angel to their 'name' . . . their 'mortal'. They can do this by leaving little gifts, notes and surprises anonymously for them. This could be a heavenly sweet like a Mars bar or heavenly words from Scripture or . . . anything within reason. These gifts are not to be expensive, on the contrary, it is more the thought than the gift that counts. Of course you can use a third party to pass on the notes or gifts. The important thing is to maintain anonymity.

Decision: You must make up your own mind whether the angels let the mortals know who they are at the end. My advice is to have a 'revealing ceremony' at one of your normal meetings or during a church service where you arrange for all the angels and mortals to be present!

Angels   Love   Fellowship   Giving

EQUIPMENT: PAPER, PENS, A HAT

⑩ Big Chip

This crowdbreaker is suitable only for big towns and cities.

The group is transported round the town in minibuses, cars, etc., surveying the local chipshops for the quality of their product. At each shop the group purchases just one bag of chips.

Prior to the outing, the young people draw up a survey sheet listing the following tests, plus any more they can think of: how greasy, how many, cost, quality of potatoes, size in terms of thickness and length, service, salt and vinegar. Have rulers, plastic plates, etc., ready for a truly professional job.

Great fun and a terrific way to meet the locals. The local newspaper may sponsor you – I'm sure they would like a picture of the testing team(s) and the result.

Make sure you return to the top chippy and present a suitable prize, decided upon by your group; something which can be signed by the testers.

Takes place outside

Judgement Testing Food Competition

EQUIPMENT: JUST MONEY!

11 Burp and Whistle

Arrange for three couples to sit in front of the group. Give each of the lads five crackers and give each of the girls a can of coke. The lads must eat the crackers as fast as possible and then whistle a tune to the satisfaction of the group; the girls must down the coke and then burp audibly.

The first couple to finish wins some crackers and another coke!

Played inside

Drinking Excitement Humour Challenge

EQUIPMENT: CRACKER BISCUITS, COKE

⊘12 Baby Burp

Arrange for three couples to volunteer! Give each girl a baby bottle filled with coke and a baby's bib. At the command to start, the girls are to sit the guys on their laps, put a bib on them and then feed the bottles to the guys. You may have to enlarge the teat holes to quicken the game. Once the bottle is empty the boy must be put over the shoulder and burped! The first one to burp is the winner.

Played inside

**Life Babies
Manners
Parenthood**

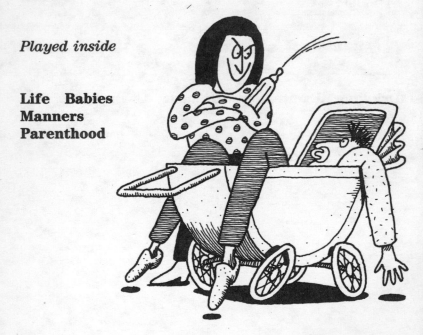

EQUIPMENT: BABY BOTTLES, COKE, BIBS

(13) Miss Match

Breaking inhibitions in any group is always difficult but this is one of our 'definites' to achieve this end.

Guys form a circle, girls form a circle inside the guys. Each person takes the person opposite as a partner. Then the guys begin to walk anti-clockwise while the girls walk clockwise. When the leader stops the music he shouts out two parts of the body, e.g. 'Eyebrow to instep!', 'Wrist to nose!', 'Knee to toe!' The new partners who now face each other get together and assume the correct position. Eliminate the slowest ones each time. Wind up with 'lip to lip!' and have a camera ready!

Played inside

Inhibitions Body Friendship Relationships Dating

My First Kiss

Choose some lads and send them out of the room. The group is told to remain entirely silent when each of the lads returns.

The first words he says will be a repeat of what he said after his first kiss, but of course he doesn't know this. One at a time, the guys come in, look around, and (we hope) say things like, 'What's going on?' 'What do I do now?'

Played inside

Embarrassment   Romance   Relationships   Deceit

EQUIPMENT: NONE

15 What — No Apples?

This crowdbreaker needs to be hyped up to make it really effective.

Volunteers are blindfolded to bob for apples in a large bowl filled with water. However, before they begin, all the apples are removed. Make sure they get a good view of the apples before the blindfolds are in place. A good volume from the audience assists in keeping the participant believing.

Variation: Get two people bobbing for non-existent apples at the same time.

Played inside

Deceit   Belief   Trust

EQUIPMENT: LARGE BOWL WITH WATER, APPLES

(16) Autograph Party

Choose two girls and two lads and get them each to remove a shoe and collect as many signatures as possible on the soles of their feet within three minutes. I will leave you to decide what type of writing instrument is to be used and how permanent the substance! No person may sign more than three feet.

The winner gets a prize, the loser is given the responsibility of trying to clean the others' feet.

Remember that in some cultures this game cannot be used.

Played inside

Pain   Hysteria   Servanthood   Losing

17 Baby, Just Smile

A person is chosen to go to anyone of the opposite sex, kneel down and say, 'If you love me, baby, just smile.'

The person must respond, 'I love you, baby, but I just can't smile,' keeping a totally straight face. If he or she begins to smile, however, the first person sits down and the other person must try to get someone else to smile. Don't let this drag, but keep it moving and make sure everyone gets a turn.

Played inside

Romance Emotions Love

EQUIPMENT: NONE

⑱ Ankle Run

Arrange for teams of no fewer than eight. The teams line up at one end of the field or room. The first person runs to a designated spot and lies down flat on his stomach. The second person straddles him and lies down ahead of him so that the first person is holding his ankles. The third person runs over both of them and lies down ahead of the second person. The next person in line can move only when the person before him hits the ground and has his ankles grabbed by the person behind.

The object is to go end-to-end all the way across the field (or round the hall) faster than the other teams. As soon as the last member of the team is flat on his stomach the first one jumps up and continues the procedure until the goal is achieved.

Why not challenge another youth group(s) to do this from one end of a football pitch to another and back again . . . if they have the energy, of course!

Variation: You can then reverse the process and do everything exactly backwards so that everyone is left standing at the end of the game.

Played inside or outside

Balance   Growth   Teamwork

EQUIPMENT: NONE

Captain O' Captain

Divide the group into three or four teams with 'captains'. They gather in opposite corners. As you call out your prepared list of items (all readily available in handbags, pockets, wallets, etc., without leaving the room), the first captain who brings you the item gets the point for his team.

Suggested Items:

> eyelash
> a false tooth
> something that proves you're failing a subject
> picture of someone's mother (this could be a £10 note)
> comb with most teeth missing
> a love letter
> 15 cm hair from a guy
> a white shoelace
> a black belt
> a 50p piece
> a left sock
> an ear-ring

Variation:

1. The captain has to ride piggy-back on one of the team members to get the item to you.

2. All the team are tied together and all have to bring the item.

Played inside

**Materialism   Enthusiasm   Leadership
Problem Solving**

20 Feather Dusters

This may be a quick crowdbreaker before another one using blindfolds. Often it is the quickie game that has a lot of punch.

Place a pair of rubber gloves on a blindfolded person. The fingers of the gloves are then daubed with shaving foam. Then quickly tickle the guy's nose with a feather.

Played inside

Deceit Fashion Surprise

EQUIPMENT: BLINDFOLDS, GLOVES, SHAVING FOAM, A FEATHER DUSTER

34

This is a great one for Europeans but not a good idea if you have young people from the Middle East, where feet are treated with more respect.

Ask everyone to remove their shoes when entering the room and leave them in a pile. Girls are then divided into two teams and turned loose to dive into the pile and emerge with a pair of guy's shoes. (If more girls are present than guys, the slow ones drop out at this point.) Each girl must then find the owner.

Next, the boy must try to find her shoes from her description or her shouts.

The winning team is the one with all the shoes on first.

Played inside

Chaos   Chance   Fashion   Tension

EQUIPMENT: NONE

22 Line Up

Get the entire group, or teams, to line up as fast as possible in the following order:

> Height
> Birthdays
> Alphabetical first names
> Alphabetical surnames
> Alphabetical grandmother's names
> Alphabetical grandfather's dog's name!
> Parent's birth date
> Teacher's surname
> House number
> Road name first letter

Played inside or outside

Competition   Courtesy   Order   Discipline

EQUIPMENT: NONE

23 Pic-Songs

Divide into teams of four to six persons each, and give each team member a number. Give each team a large piece of paper and a felt-tip pen or crayon.

Then call all the number 1s up to get the title of a current song. They rush back to their respective teams and draw pictures (no words) until the other members guess the title. As soon as they get it, number 2s rush up and the process repeats.

The first team to get all 10 songs wins the opportunity to sing to the rest. Don't mention this until you get a winner!

Played inside

Music   Creativity   Communication

EQUIPMENT: PAPER, FELT-TIP PENS

(24) Balloon Scramble

Ideal for Christmas, Valentine's Day or a party!

Decorate a room with clusters of balloons tied to streamers. Each balloon contains a small slip of paper with a number on it.

At some point during the evening, tell the group that there are numbers inside the balloons and that some of them are worth prizes. Then pull down the streamers, and watch the scramble.

When all the balloons have been burst and the numbers retrieved, call on the winners and give crazy as well as valuable prizes.

Variation: For a Valentine's party, get each person to write something romantic on a small piece of paper and fold it up small. These should be pushed through the neck into the balloon before blowing up. At a suitable moment the balloons are popped one at a time to reveal the message.

Played inside

Christmas   Valentine Party   Choice   Relationships Love

EQUIPMENT: BALLOONS

25 Love Balloons

This is one of those thoughtful games which unless you have created the correct atmosphere can become a disaster in the first degree. You have been warned!

At the end of a study, say on 1 Corinthians 13 (love) or Galatians 5:22 (fruit of the Spirit), get the young people to write on small pieces of paper a verse appropriate to themselves which could become a gift verse for somebody else. Each paper is rolled up carefully and slotted through the neck of a balloon, then the balloon is blown up and tied. At a suitable time later, each person chooses a balloon and bursts it open to receive a verse.

Played inside

Bible   Love   Fruit of the Spirit

EQUIPMENT: BALLOONS, PAPER, PENS

Toss pieces of unused bubble gum to the young people, enough for one each. The last person to blow a bubble gets to volunteer for the next game!

Variation: The biggest bubble
The loudest bang
The rudest noise

Played inside

Rudeness   Embarrassment   Competition   Humour

EQUIPMENT: BUBBLE GUM

27 Natural Sounds

This one is useful for any situation where a large group needs to be broken into smaller groups.

Pass out slips of paper reading: bath time, toe-nail cutting, gargling, electric razors, sleeping, hair dryers, tooth brushes. Then turn out the lights and have kids make the sound of their team (singing, clip clip ouch, gargle, buzzzz, snores, hum, ch-ch-ch, respectively) as they try to find the other team members.

Played inside

Teamwork   Guidance   Chaos   Church

EQUIPMENT: SLIPS OF PAPER

(28) Smelly Socks

All the young people remove their shoes. When the lights are turned off, everyone gathers as many socks as possible. Allow about two minutes of darkness, with a quick flicker in the middle.

This can also be a team game with points for the net gain in number of socks collected. You must know your group very well for this one and everyone needs to be wearing trousers.

Played inside

Servanthood   Losing   Failure   Fashion

Persuaders

Volunteer two or three guys to leave the room.

Blindfold them and bring them back one at a time to listen to two girls trying to coax them to move in their direction.

Tell the guy that one of the persuaders has a penalty (a shaving cream pie to throw) while the other has a reward (a kiss or sweet).

He must decide within two minutes, on the basis of the girls' persuasive powers and their sincerity, which way to move.

This crowdbreaker goes very well if the two girls play their part. You may want to brief them beforehand for maximum impact.

Played inside

Relationships Sex Persuasion Lying Punishment Reward Deceit

EQUIPMENT: SHAVING FOAM, BLINDFOLDS

30 Tight Fit

Sit two guys on chairs in front of the rest. After taking off their shoes and socks they are blindfolded and given thick garden gloves to wear.

Then each one of them is given a pair of tights. The winner is the first guy to get them up over his knees.

Arrange the necessary cheering for this event.

Variation: On completion of the initial task the guy has to walk the full length of the room and back with a book on his head.

Played inside

Homosexuality Fashion Difficulties Roles

EQUIPMENT: BLINDFOLDS, GARDEN GLOVES, TIGHTS

(31) Interesting!

Send two or three young people out of the room. Have your assistant tell them you are going to interview them about their interests. They are not to identify their interests, but simply answer the questions, and the crowd will guess which hobby is being described.

While they are gone, tell the group that your questions refer not at all to their interests but to kissing. Bring them in all together and play the interview as straight as you can, asking question 1 to all of them before proceeding to question 2.

1. How old were you when you first did this?
2. Who taught you how?
3. Is there someone you really like to do this with?
4. Where do you usually do it?
5. Is there a particular time of day when you like to do this?
6. When you do this, what kind of sound does it make?
7. How many people have you done this with?

Played inside

Relationships Dating Embarrassment

EQUIPMENT: NONE

45

Tie strings of liquorice together to make strings approximately two metres long.

Use as many couples as you wish. Give a string to each couple and instruct them to start at opposite ends and eat until they meet.

Any couple breaking its string is automatically disqualified.

A camera at the ready is essential if you want to use it against them at a later date!

Variation: Have the strings cross like the spokes of a wheel and watch the fun.

Played inside

Greed   Attraction   Church

EQUIPMENT: LOTS AND LOTS OF 'STRING LIQUORICE'

33 Ladies and Gentlemen . . .

Choose four extra-extroverts and take them out of the room.

Bring them back one at a time and give each 50 seconds to make a sales pitch for an item which you hold in a sack.

You and the crowd know what it is (last year's diary, a toothbrush or a comb), but the salesman does not.

After the sales pitch, let the crowd ask the salesman questions about the usefulness and quality of the item.

After all four have performed, vote for the best salesman.

Played inside

Gospel Communication Consumerism Materialism Peer Pressure

EQUIPMENT: SACK OF OBJECTS

(34) Mummies and Daddies

Get two couples to volunteer (a boy and a girl) and stand them back to back.

Each pair is given a roll of toilet paper. Together, they try to do the best job at wrapping themselves into a single mummy. The crowd judges at the end.

Variation: Two groups of three or four people, in which case maybe two toilet rolls will be required!

Played inside

History   Evidence   Death   Parenthood

EQUIPMENT: TOILET PAPER

35 Building Without Hands

Put several cardboard boxes of various sizes (very large and very wee) in the middle of the room.

Select two or more couples to compete at stacking the boxes into one vertical column as quickly as possible without using their hands.

Time each couple, to decide on the winners.

The winners should receive a gift in a presentation box for their efforts.

Variation: The couples use only their feet!

Played inside

Cooperation   Church   Individuality

EQUIPMENT: BOXES

36 Bet You Can't!

A couple of young people are directed to stand against a wall.

They must pin both shoulders against the wall and the outside edge of one shoe. When you say 'Go!' they are to lift the other leg into the air. It is impossible, but the contortions of trying to do it are entertaining.

Played inside

Gambling   Will Power   Body Movements

EQUIPMENT: NONE

37 Time!

Bring two people to the front and give each a cheap alarm clock, a screwdriver, a pair of pliers and any other tools you wish.

Tell each of them to take the clock apart without breaking anything.

The person with the most separated parts at the end of four minutes wins.

Variation:

1. Have two people put it together again – they may need longer than four minutes!
2. Have two teams; each person must take a part of the activity by unscrewing a part or by adding a part of the clock.
3. If you really want to be a masochist, give each person some large gardening or kitchen gloves to wear.

Played inside

Patience Teamwork Time Church Fellowship

EQUIPMENT: DISCARDED CLOCKS, SCREWDRIVERS, PLIERS

38 Volleyball Hop

This is a guys versus girls volleyball game (use lots and lots of players), with one notable change: each guy has his ankles tied together with cloth.

Tie the cloth a little slack so they can shuffle along or hop like a kangaroo, but not enough to give them an advantage.

Variation: Basketball hop.

Played inside or outside

Teamwork   Sexuality   Balance   Friendship

EQUIPMENT: BALL, LENGTHS OF CLOTH

(39) Flash in the Dark

Make the room totally dark and use a flashing strobe light.

Have two people stand 3 or 4 metres apart and give them a pillow to toss back and forth.

If, when the strobe light is on (at a slow speed, which makes it all the more difficult), they can complete three tosses back and forth without getting hit in the face, they are amazing!

Warning: Remember stroboscopes used at high frequencies can be dangerous. Control of the equipment is your responsibility.

Played inside

Darkness   Abilities   Light

EQUIPMENT: STROBES, CUSHION OR PILLOW

40 All Heart

Prepare a large cardboard or wooden heart which rests on an easel.

Paint it red and add a few smallish white circles. Use enamel paint as arrows will need to stick to it.

At the meeting, call two dating couples to the front. Give each guy a child's bow and three arrows with rubber suction ends.

Each arrow that sticks on the heart earns three points; each arrow that sticks on a white circle earns five points.

After three rounds of shooting (nine shots total per guy), add up the score and reward the winner. Tease the loser by saying that his girl friend is probably a better shot than he is. As his penalty, he is going to have to play William Tell. Place an apple on his head and let the girl fire away. (Clue both girls ahead of time to be sure to miss intentionally – aim for the floor, or shoot way over his head. Otherwise, it can be dangerous!)

Played inside or outside

Romance   Cupid   Judgement

EQUIPMENT: A HEART, TWO CHILDREN'S BOWS,
ARROWS WITH RUBBER SUCTION ENDS

41 Body Spell

Select two pairs to compete in spelling out a phrase to the group a letter at a time.

They must form the letters with their bodies (e.g. leaning toward each other with heads touching and arms extended to make an 'A'). No fingers may be used to form individual letters. Give each pair a simple phrase like 'blow your nose'.

Variation: Have teams with two people from each running to you as the coordinator for words or phrases that they must act out to their team. Once the team has guessed correctly, two more then take a turn in acting out the letters. Charades with a difference!

Played inside

Roles   Drama   Education

EQUIPMENT: NONE

42 Burn-up

Organize a track round the floor, making sure it zig-zags round and under furniture.

Two or more persons must each push a toy car round the track with their noses.

You can determine the winner by timing them or seeing who comes in first. Make sure you have a chequered flag to signal the winner.

The loser is presented with a plastic false nose to wear for the rest of the evening.

Played inside

Competition   Time   Co-ordination

EQUIPMENT: TOY CARS AND TRACK

43 Oscars All Round

At a retreat or some special event, have someone take video footage.

Edit this if you have the technique or equipment and show it at a subsequent meeting.

Make up a story line to go with the video, or let people fill in with comments as they view it. Slow down the footage, run it backwards, do anything that will make it funny.

Variation: Give them two hours to produce a five-minute not-so-serious drama on the given theme of the retreat. Video it. Play it back and allow the wails and screams. Everyone must play a part in the movie! If it's a large group, split them up and make a competition of it. Present 'Oscars' to the winners.

Played inside or outside

Drama   Life   Emotion   Pride

EQUIPMENT: VIDEO CAMERA

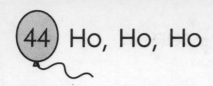

44 Ho, Ho, Ho

This is a great favourite of ours. One of the best in this book.

Use as many of your young people as you wish. The first one lies on the floor on his back. The second lies at right angles to the first with his head on the first person's stomach, the third does the same and so on until you have a long line.

Once they are all in position, ask the first person to say with some feeling, 'Ho, ho, ho!' The second person follows by adding another 'ho' (making four 'ho, ho's'). The third person now begins and adds another 'ho' and so on all down the line. Before long they and the onlookers will be laughing uncontrollably.

Variation: As above except that you announce to them all how many 'ho, ho's' they all say together. Either way don't plan anything too seriously immediately after this crowdbreaker. Everyone will be hurting too much.

Played inside

Christmas Laughter Fun

EQUIPMENT: NONE

(45) Musical Disasters

Pass a bag of clothes around the circle. Whenever the music stops, the person holding the bag must immediately reach in and pull out the first thing he touches and wear it for the rest of the evening.

Cram the bag with weird things: old T-shirts, girdles, lipstick, floppy sweaters, large socks, baggy pants, curlers, large ear-rings (clip-on) etc.

Played inside

Fashion   Families   Church(!)

EQUIPMENT: A SACK OF WEIRD AND COLOURFUL CLOTHES

46 Target Practice

Place a big blob of shaving cream on the nose of one or more guys.

Line up an equal number of girls about 3 metres away and equip each with a water pistol. The girl who gets the shaving cream off the nose first, wins the prize: her guy gets first use of the water pistol, this time on the youth leader!

Played inside or outside

War   Violence   Suffering   Tension

EQUIPMENT: SHAVING CREAM, WATER PISTOLS OR
PLASTIC WASHING-UP LIQUID CONTAINERS

Freeze a pound coin in each of several VERY large ice blocks.

Give each team an ice block and a wooden spoon. The first team to get to its money can keep it; the others have to give it back.

If you can arrange for the ice cubes to come from an industrial freezer then you could be looking at a one metre ice cube . . . try for it!

Played inside or outside

Frustration   Coldness   Money

EQUIPMENT: SEVERAL POUND COINS, WOODEN SPOONS

(48) Ice Chest

This is an old favourite which always breaks the ice!

Provide two of the more extrovert and 'have a go at anything' lads with very large shirts and ask for two girls to volunteer. Shirts must be tucked in very well – even tied round the waist if a strong belt is not worn.

Each girl is given a very large bag of ice cubes which she must stuff, a handful at a time, down the guy's neck in front and back.

This is one of the worst crowdbreakers in this book but one of the best!

Played inside or outside

Tension Feeeeeeeelings! Consequences Control

EQUIPMENT: ICE

(49) Prune Feed

This is a disgusting crowdbreaker and one that defies imagination and therefore one to be played!

Volunteer three guys and three girls.

Each of the guys is to lie at the feet of a girl. Each girl is given a set number of prunes and feeds her guy using only her feet. The winning couple watches the other couples reverse roles so that the guys feed the girls!

Warning: Those eating the prunes must not lie on their backs but on their sides or fronts.

Played inside

Food   Co-operation   Babies   Families

EQUIPMENT: PRUNES

50 Marbles on Ice

This crowdbreaker is excellent for a cold evening.

Six marbles are placed in a large bucket of ice. Your volunteers are each timed to get all the marbles out using just a bare foot.

A marble cannot be lifted out by jamming it between the bucket and foot. It must be carefully and coolly brought out between the toes.

Beat our record of 18 seconds if you can!

Played inside

Abilities   Control   Culture   Manners

EQUIPMENT: MARBLES, ICE, A BUCKET

51 A Messy End

The youth leader gives an impressive speech about his ability to guess accurately the weight of any person, simply by lifting the person.

Each person sits on the floor with his knees drawn up and arms locked underneath. The youth leader then leans over from behind and locks his hands under the person's knees as well, enabling him to lift the person all at once. He then asks for volunteers, promising to get within one kilogram of the correct answers.

Each volunteer informs the audience of his weight by writing it on a large piece of paper while the youth leader closes his eyes.

The first two volunteers, however, have been clued ahead of time and have told the youth leader their weights, so naturally he gets the first two right.

The third volunteer is naive; he is lifted and then set down in a tray of shaving foam placed under him by a friend from behind.

Messy game but great!

Played inside or outside

Friendship   Deceit   Lying   Cheating   Sin

EQUIPMENT: SHAVING FOAM, TRAY

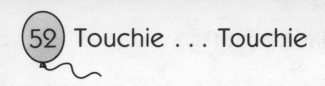

52 Touchie . . . Touchie

This is a simple and easy fill-in.

Place your chosen objects in the centre of two teams and see which team can get the most members touching their object in any way by any method.

The jam-up will need to be cut off after 60 seconds or so; then the count begins. (If you think this might get too rough, play it with guys only and then girls only.)

Played inside

Selfishness   Violence   Winning

EQUIPMENT: ANY TWO OBJECTS

(53) Trial By Egg

This needs building up, so as you lay out a trail of eggs explain how they must walk very carefully between them.

Naturally they will think this is easy and wonder why the build-up was so strong. Then you announce that each person will be blindfolded.

Volunteer three people of the screaming, squeamish type and bring them in one at a time, blindfolded.

Meanwhile you or your assistants have removed the eggs and replaced them with piles of cornflakes. Each volunteer must walk slowly across the eggs (cornflakes) and each time they tread on a pile the crowd must make the appropriate noises!

This is a great one that deserves the speeches beforehand.

Have a camera ready for when you take off the blindfold at the end and they review their feet and then the 'eggs'!

Played inside or outside

Tension Food Trust Deceit Scheming

EQUIPMENT: EGGS, CORNFLAKES, PLASTIC SHEETING

54 Drop It!

For this crowdbreaker you must face the consequences if it gets out of hand!

One person lies on the floor with hands outstretched. A second person holds a raw egg over his head at chest height. The person on the floor may move his hands to catch the egg as soon as it is released. If he's too slow, he gets it in the face. If he's too fast and catches it with too much enthusiasm, he may wish he had missed.

Warning: It may be good to have some plastic sheeting and a towel around for this one!

Played inside or outside

Tension Enthusiasm
Consequences Food
Abilities Chance

EGG OF THE GIANT ORC

EQUIPMENT: RAW EGGS

55 Choose Your Weapon

Two blindfolded young people hold a lighted candle in one hand, a water pistol in the other.

The first to extinguish the other person's candle is the winner. The candle and water pistol should be held about 1.5 metres apart.

Warning: Be careful to make safety your priority.

Variations: make two hats using aluminium foil baking trays. Partly melt a candle on each so that they 'stick', and attach elastic bands to hold the tray on the head. Two young people stand two metres apart with water pistols at the ready and attempt to douse each other's candle. They do not need blindfolds for this variation.

I have never seen this one fail to get the desired effect!

Played inside or outside

War   Violence   Resources   Darkness

EQUIPMENT: WATER PISTOLS, CANDLES, BLINDFOLDS

56) It's the Pits!

Organize two teams of six and seat them in front of a table of food.

The food must be wrapped and numbered, and members of the team draw lots out of a hat to discover their delicacy.

Some are pleasant (apple pie, chocolate bar, shredded wheat), others are harder to take (raw onion, jar of baby food, large gherkin). The first team (not individual member) to down all its food in sequence wins a prize (Alka-Seltzer!).

Variation: Blindfold three persons and feed them one at a time with different foods, simple and difficult. They have to identify each one. The winner gets a rare supermarket fruit.

Played inside

Food Chance Choice Hunger Suffering Third World

EQUIPMENT: VARIOUS FOODS

57 Michelangelo

Purchase some oblong packets of firm margarine and keep in the refrigerator at a very low temperature.

Bring these out of the cold just before the crowdbreaker and volunteer three people to sculpt the blocks in front of the group.

You choose the subject matter – a straight head and shoulders is most likely to be recognizable!

Played inside

God   Creativity   Image   Design

EQUIPMENT: MARGARINE, KNIVES

58 Epitaphs

Everyone has looked round tombstones sometime and seen funny or profound epitaphs.

Get your group to write funny or profound epitaphs for themselves.

Then they are to pass the papers with their ideas on to you for you to read out. The group has to guess the author of each one.

An example of a profound epitaph: 'New address, please see John 14:2.'

Played inside

Death Epitaphs Heaven Hell Life

EQUIPMENT: PAPER, PENS

59 A Present Surprise

Each person is to bring a carefully wrapped present to the value of £1 to your group meeting. It is important that you explain that it should be a gift that either sex would appreciate.

You should have a couple spare for those who forget.

As part of your programme, and while music is playing, get everyone to shake hands with someone and then circulate round the room. When the music stops, each person should return to the person with whom they shook hands.

They should exchange presents and then open them. After the expected 'wows', moans and other suitable noises, announce that they must now get into a circle.

Once they are organized, drop the bombshell that they should now pass their presents to the person five places to their left. This time they can keep their presents!

Played inside

Choice   Chance   Gambling   Gifts   Giving

EQUIPMENT: PRESENTS, MUSIC

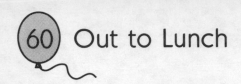

60 Out to Lunch

What signs would various shops hang on the door to create a smile among the readers?

Put your group into twos and threes and give them this exercise: write lunchtime 'out to lunch' signs which are both humorous and relate to what the shop sells.

Give them two or three examples from below:

Garden centre:	Gone to pot!
Yachting club:	Gone to the wind!
Fortune-teller:	Back in the future!
Music shop:	Gone Chopin! Back in a minuet!
Boatyard:	Gone for launch!
Kindergarten:	Gone for din-dins!
Watchmaker:	Back in a tick!
Fishmonger:	Pulled a muscle!
Launderette:	Got a pressing engagement!
Woolshop:	Unwinding!
Hairdresser:	Curled up for an hour!

Played inside

Communication   Humour   Attitudes

EQUIPMENT: PENS, PAPER

61 Cornflakes Dip

This is a yukkkkkky one in the extreme but worth every inch of camera film. It will be discussed for a long time.

Set up a bowl of syrup, not too deep (a cereal bowl is fine), and drop a polo mint into the middle. Seek volunteers to scoop out the polo mint with their mouths. The syrup must be deep enough for the person to get the gooey mess all round the mouth and cheeks and chin!

Once successful the lucky volunteer must immediately attempt to scoop another polo mint out of a large bowl of cornflakes.

Whether they succeed or not is almost irrelevent . . . although it's to be encouraged.

The sight of the unfortunate participant rising from the cornflakes is one for the youth annals of history!

Played inside or outside

Cleanliness   Achievement   Looks

EQUIPMENT: CORNFLAKES, GOLDEN SYRUP, POLO MINTS, A TOWEL, BOWLS — AND WASHING FACILITIES!

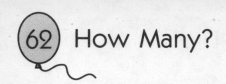

62 How Many?

The key to this crowdbreaker is your use of the spoons, which in fact have nothing to do with the activity! Confused? Good, we can now proceed.

Take six spoons – the size is irrelevant – and place them in any pattern you like, touching or otherwise. Make a big play on this and 'hum' and 'ha' as to whether they are quite right. Even change one of them slightly to give the impression that it was not quite in the right place.

Then ask your group, 'How many?' Not how many spoons but simply, 'how many?' Naturally your group will think you are referring to the spoons, but in reality it is how many fingers on both your hands are being discreetly displayed.

The group will guess how many (spoons). After a few guesses you say the correct answer which will probably be different from most guesses.

Display and request their guesses several times before their frustration leads them to lynch you. Some may guess, and you ask them to keep quiet or to display the spoons on your behalf.

Do not give away your secret, but move on quickly to another crowdbreaker or subject.

Played inside

Frustration Magic Participation Evidence Understanding

EQUIPMENT: SPOONS

63 Scissor Wrap

This crowdbreaker is very similar to number 62 in that it relies on what is understood and not on the reality! We are not getting too philosophical . . . you will understand all.

Sit everyone round in a circle, preferably on chairs, though this is not essential.

Pass round the circle a pair of scissors. Each time it is handed on, you declare it 'open' or 'closed'. This is irrelevant to whether it is true or not, as the statements relate in reality to whether the receiver's legs are crossed or not.

For example, the person next to me in the circle to whom I am passing the scissors may have his legs crossed. So I may pass the open scissors to him and say 'closed', because in reality I am referring to his legs and not to the scissors at all!

To his surprise the next time round, if his legs are still crossed, I may pass the scissors to him again and say 'closed' – which is likely to baffle him and everyone participating even more.

Do not reveal the secret, and stop once you have been round the circle two or three times.

Played inside

Frustration   Secrets   Evidence   Revelation

EQUIPMENT: SCISSORS

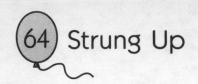

64 Strung Up

You must know your group reasonably well to have the confidence to do this and be assured that everyone will participate. Also you must be happy about the clothing each person is wearing.

The spoon is tied to a very long piece of soft but unbreakable string.

Two teams stand in line and on the signal to begin the first person drops the spoon down his or her shirt/blouse and down through the trousers. The string is pulled through to enable the next person to repeat the process, and so on until the whole team is 'strung up', or rather 'strung down'.

Variation: You can of course reverse the game so that the process is repeated backwards. You can also use their predicament to play your next crowdbreaker all strung together . . . can get painful.

Played inside

Church   Fellowship   Teamwork

EQUIPMENT: SPOONS, STRING

65 Bottoms Up

This is definitely an outside crowdbreaker with all the fun of it going totally wrong . . . you hope!

In teams of about eight people, they are to lie down in a circle with their feet up in the air.

As the leader you carefully balance a plastic bucket filled with water onto the feet of the participants – who keep it there for sheer fear that it could overturn on them.

Once the bucket is carefully balanced and everyone is giggling nervously, then ask them all to take off their shoes and socks one person at a time. Then stand back and let it all happen!

Played outside

Excitement Tension Baptism Teamwork Fear Laughter

EQUIPMENT: A BUCKET, LOTS OF WATER!

RECIPES

No-Cook Chocolate Biscuit Cake

4 oz margarine
8 oz chopped cooking chocolate
4 tbspn golden syrup
8 oz petit beurre type biscuits (crumbled)
2 oz desiccated coconut

Melt the margarine, chocolate and syrup in a saucepan. Stir in biscuits and coconut. Spoon into two greased shallow 15cm (6 inch) square cake tins and press firmly, using the cut side of an orange.

Leave to set, then cut into squares.

Lemon Fingers

These are wonderful for people living in hot countries and for those days when the cooker packs up or for economizing on fuel bills!

8 oz digestive biscuits (crushed)
1 cup desiccated coconut
rind of 1 lemon
4 oz butter
½ tin condensed milk

Icing
1¾ cups icing sugar
½ oz butter
2 tbspn lemon juice

Melt butter and mix in remaining ingredients. Press into a greased swiss-roll tin and place in the fridge.

When set, mix icing ingredients together, spread over cake, and cut into squares.

Flapjacks

8 oz oats
6 oz butter
6 oz brown sugar
a pinch of salt

Melt the butter and stir in the sugar, salt and oats.

Turn the mixture into a shallow greased baking tray and press flat.

Bake for 20 to 30 minutes in a moderately hot oven.

Mark into squares while warm, but leave to cool before removing them from the tray.

If you wish, cover with melted chocolate for sheer irresistibility.

Coconut Biscuits

5 oz soft margarine
1 egg
8 oz self-raising flour
5 oz caster sugar
4 oz desiccated coconut

Mix all the ingredients together.

Roll out and cut with cutter.

Place on a greased baking tray.

Cook in a moderate oven for 25 minutes.

Melting Moments

4 oz margarine
3 oz sugar
5 oz self-raising flour
½ egg
cooking chocolate buttons
rolled oats

Beat fat and sugar well, then beat in the egg.

Stir in the flour and add chocolate (as much as you like).

Roll the mixture into balls and dip each one in water, then coat with oats.

Place on a greased tray.

Bake in a moderate oven for 15–20 minutes.

(I usually double this recipe to use the other half egg.)

Carrot Cake

In a large mixing bowl:

Beat until creamy: 2 cups sugar
                              4 egg yolks
                              1½ cups oil

Sift: 2 cups self-raising flour
                              2 teaspoons baking powder
                              1 teaspoon salt

Mix all ingredients
together with: 1 cup of grated carrot
                              1 cup of chopped nuts

Whisk 4 egg whites until stiff and fold them into the mixture.

Pour into a large greased loaf tin and bake in a moderate oven for about one hour.

Ice with butter icing mixed with a little coffee and sprinkle chopped nuts on top.

This recipe is also ideal as a chocolate cake. Replace ¼ cup of flour with cocoa and leave out the nuts. Ice with chocolate butter icing or melted cooking chocolate.

These cakes are always a hit. Make sure they are cooked long enough to avoid them being too gooey! Cooking it in a large roasting tin reduces cooking time and makes it easier to cut.

Ramsden and Ramsden
SKETCHES

The Three Bears

by Ramsden and Ramsden

Setting the scene:
A girl (mother) sitting in an armchair with a book as if to read to the audience (of children!). The detectives come on in any detective outfit they would prefer, so long as it is larger than life!

Story-teller: There were three bears who . . .

1st Detective: (Cutting in) Why were there only three?

Story-teller: I don't know, there just were three bears who . . .

2nd Detective: But why were there only three? Answer the question.

Story-teller: Because there were three, that's all.

1st Detective: Are you absolutely sure?

Story-teller: Yes.

2nd Detective: But you can't tell us why?

Story-teller: Look, I'm telling you, there were only three because that's the way it was.

1st D: But why three?

S.T.:   I don't know.

2nd D: So now you don't know.

1st D: So you lied earlier?

S.T.:   Look, I don't know why there were three. I don't know, I don't know.

2nd D: You don't know very much, do you?

S.T.:   Please, leave me alone! There was a mummy bear, a daddy bear and a baby bear.

1st D: So there's a baby involved?

91

2nd D:	Why didn't you tell us before?
S.T.:	You didn't ask.
1st D:	That is not a valid answer. I demand to know why there were only three bears and why you didn't tell us that there was a child involved.
2nd D:	Why did they only have one kid?
S.T.:	I don't know!
1st D:	Were there mental problems?
2nd D:	Were they separated?
S.T.:	How am I supposed to know? I'm only telling a story.
1st D:	So, just to recap, there were three bears.
2nd D:	Just three bears.
1st D:	Not one, not five or ten, but three?
S.T.:	Like I said before, just three.
2nd D:	So, we have a daddy bear who is possibly having an affair, a mother bear who is lazy, and a baby bear who is very possibly mentally disturbed.
S.T.:	I didn't say that.
1st D:	But it's implied, isn't it? Can you tell us for certain that this was not the case?
S.T.:	No.
1st D:	Well then, it seems to me that your story is missing some vital facts.
S.T.:	Can I continue?
2nd D:	Very well, tell us, without admitting anything that may be used in a court of law.
S.T.:	The three bears went for a walk in the woods and . . .
1st D:	So, you're still insisting that there were only three bears?
S.T.:	Good grief.

92

2nd D:	Why?
S.T.:	I'm sorry.
1st D:	Not as sorry as you're going to be, mate. (Story-teller puts his face in his hands.)
2nd D:	Why did they go into the woods?
S.T.:	I told you, for a walk.
1st D:	Do you think it's wise to let a family with a psychotic child loose in the woods?
S.T.:	Look, they went for a walk so that their porridge could cool down.
2nd D:	What porridge?
S.T.:	The porridge they were going to eat for breakfast.
1st D:	Do you think a 250kg bear will be satisfied after eating *one* bowl of porridge?
S.T.:	Well, yes.
2nd D:	Do you now claim to be an expert dietician on the habitual eating habits of bears? Never mind answering that, just continue with the story.
S.T.:	While they were away, Goldilocks . . .
1st D:	Who?
S.T.:	Goldilocks.
2nd D:	Was she a blonde?
S.T.:	No.
1st D:	Then why on earth was she called Goldilocks?
S.T.:	Because that's what her parents christened her as.
2nd D:	Were Goldy's parents psychopaths too?
S.T.:	No!
1st D:	Then why did they give her a name that rhymes with smelly-socks?
S.T.:	Look, the bears went for a walk . . .
2nd D:	Just three . . .

S.T.:	And Goldilocks walked into their house and . . .
1st D:	So, breaking and entering. The plot thickens. What did she do, smash down the door with an axe, or perhaps she forced the lock with her American Express card.
S.T.:	What American Express card?
2nd D:	Make a note of that. She didn't have any credit cards. Probably got a long history of bad debts.
S.T.:	Please!
1st D:	What now?
S.T.:	Look, Goldilocks was not a thief, she was just a . . .
2nd D:	Kleptomaniac. I've come across these characters before. Very dangerous. I'll put out an A.P.B. for her arrest.
1st D:	I'm slightly confused. Where does Cinderella come into all this?
2nd D:	Yeah, and what about this dude, Rumpelstiltskin?
S.T.:	That's a different story.
1st D:	But these things are always interconnected.
2nd D:	Let me tell you the story, you correct me when I go wrong. The three bears went for a walk, Goldilocks forces her way into the house by bulldozing down the front door with a tractor, the three bears run back to the house armed with spears and swords. Goldilocks' accomplice, Jack, cuts down the giant beanstalk which falls on the three bears killing them instantly. Jack and Goldilocks then make a clean get-away with the family jewels. Right?

S.T.:	No!
2nd D:	Then we are going to keep telling it to you until we do get it right. Come with us. (As they leave stage) There was this mermaid who lived on the bottom of the ocean . . .

The Three Little Pigs

by Ramsden and Ramsden

Setting the scene: the same as 'The Three Bears'

S.T.:	Once upon a time, there were three little pigs.
1st D:	How old were they?
S.T.:	I'm sorry?
2nd D:	You don't know how old they were?
S.T.:	Well, it's not really important, is it!
1st D:	It's up to us to decide what's important or not, just give us the facts.
S.T.:	I'm trying to! There were three little pigs who went off to build houses and . . .
2nd D:	Not so fast. So these little pigs have left home, have they?
S.T.:	I suppose so.
1st D:	In which case the age of the pigs is very important.
S.T.:	I can't see why.
2nd D:	Supposing they weren't pigs at all. Supposing they were . . . piglets.
1st D:	Minors who have been forcibly evicted from their home. That would explain why they were so little.
S.T.:	Look, it's not that important.
2nd D:	Deliberately withholding information, that is two to three years already. Now, how old were the pigs?
S.T.:	I don't know.
1st D:	Where did the pigs' parents live?

S.T.:	Pardon me?
2nd D:	You heard the question.
S.T.:	I don't see what this has to do with . . .
1st D:	Listen, unless we get some co-operation fast, things are going to get nasty. Where are the pigs' parents?
S.T.:	How am I supposed to know? I'm only telling a story.
2nd D:	Okay, so we have three juvenile delinquent piglets, evicted from their home by a psychotic father and uncaring mother. Thcy are armed and therefore are very possibly dangerous. I'll put out an A.P.B. for their arrest.
S.T.:	A what?
1st and 2nd D:	A warrant, Gertrude.
1st D:	So we have three piglets with disturbed childhoods. Going to build houses you say; missile silos, more like it.
S.T.:	Please let me tell the story. The pigs build their houses when this big wolf . . .
2nd D:	You mean a lawyer?
S.T.:	I said wolf.
2nd D:	I heard you.
1st D:	Wait a minute, wait a minute. Is this the same wolf that was involved in the case of Red Riding Hood?
S.T.:	That's another story.
2nd D:	These things are always interconnected! How many times must we tell you?
S.T.:	I'm telling *you*, there were two different wolves.
1st D:	How do you know? Can you give a positive description of each wolf? Names, addresses, shoe size . . .
S.T.:	Shoe size? You must be joking!

2nd D:	In other words you have no tangible evidence whatsoever to prove that we are talking about two separate wolves. Things are starting to look very bad for you.
1st D:	What do you know about the Red Riding Hood case then?
S.T.:	Well, Little Red Riding Hood . . .
2nd D:	*Little, Little* Red Riding Hood! Another juvenile! Make a note of that, Little Red Riding Hood was under-age at the time of the incident.
1st D:	Do you think she could have been a piglet in disguise?
2nd D:	Yeah, yeah. Plastic surgery, anything is possible these days. Make a note of that.
S.T.:	You people stop at nothing, do you. Listen, she was going to see her grandmother when . . .
1st D:	Grandmother! Pimp more like it.
S.T.:	A what? I don't believe this. The grandmother was a good guy, it was the wolf who . . .
1st D:	That's it, you admitted it. 'The grandmother was a good guy,' i.e. the grandmother was actually a man running a brothel down 52nd Street. The wolf, this lawyer fellow, falls in love with Little Red Riding Hood who works for the grandmother as a car mechanic and part-time prostitute. The grandmother finds out about the wolf's intentions to take Little Red Riding Hood away, and puts out a contract for the wolf's assassination. Little Red Riding Hood's elder brother, Robin Hood, together with his merry men, agree to kill the lawyer . . .

S.T.:	I don't believe this. Look, can I tell you the rest of my story? Thank you! Now, the wolf goes to the first piglet's house and demands that he be let in or else he will blow the house down.
2nd D:	You mean up.
S.T.:	What?
2nd D:	You mean he will blow the house up, not down.
1st D:	Tell me, was the wolf a vegetarian?
S.T.:	Good grief – I'm going insane, of course the wolf wasn't a vegetarian.
2nd D:	Aha! So you know what this wolf likes to eat. That implies that you know this lawyer very well. What is his address?
S.T.:	Not that again?
1st D:	What?
S.T.:	That!
2nd D:	Where?
S.T.:	Here!
1st D:	There?
2nd D:	Here?
S.T.:	What did you say?
1st D:	. . . What? That! Where? Here! There! Here! (FAST)
S.T.:	Someone get me a doctor, I'm losing my mind.
2nd D:	What, here?
1st D:	She's there!
2nd D:	Where?
S.T.:	Please, I beg of you, anything but that (suffering from a nervous breakdown) (1st and 2nd D shake hands)
2nd D:	So now, let's start from the beginning, leaving nothing out. So we have this wizard, Merlin (S.T. collapses)

Title Index

Subject Index

Romance, 26, 29, 54
Rudeness, 40

Scheming, 67
Second Coming of Christ, 18
Servanthood, 28, 42
Sex, 43
Sexuality, 52
Sharing, 14
Sin, 65
Suffering, 60, 70
Surprise, 34

Teamwork, 41, 51, 52, 78, 79

Tension, 35, 60, 62, 67, 68, 79
Terror, 18
Testing, 22
Third World, 70
Time, 51, 56
Trust, 27, 67

Understanding, 76

Valentine, 38
Violence, 60, 66, 69

War, 60, 69
Will power, 50

Inside or Outside Index

Inside: 11, 12, 25, 26, 27, 28, 30, 32, 33, 35, 36, 37, 38, 39, 40, 41, 42, 43, 44, 45, 46, 47, 48, 49, 50, 51, 52, 53, 54, 55, 56, 57, 58, 59, 60, 61, 62, 63, 64, 65, 66, 67, 68, 69, 70, 71, 72, 73, 74, 75, 76, 77, 78

Outside: 11, 15, 17, 18, 19, 29, 52, 54, 60, 61, 65, 67, 68, 69, 75, 79

Note: Most of the 'Inside' crowdbreakers can be played 'outside' when the weather allows.